Spirit of Truth

Finding certainty and standing firm in a troubled world

THE TEN COMMANDMENTS SERIES

Marja Verschoor-Meijers

Jesus answered. "You say that I am a king. I was born and came into the world for this one purpose, to speak about the truth. Whoever belongs to the truth listens to Me."

"And what is truth?" Pilate asked.

John 18:37-38

Table of contents

Introduction

Do not accuse anyone falsely.

Exodus 20:16

One of the most famous questions ever asked in the history of mankind, was the one Pilate desperately confronted Jesus with: *And what is truth?* As long as the earth exists people have been looking for truth; mankind has searched for that one certainty that would settle all disputes, all error, all doubt: truth!

For centuries, the 9th commandment has taught Christians and probably non-Christians alike, not to accuse anyone falsely. It seems such a simple act of kindness; be nice to everyone and don't lie. However, today we live in a world that seems to be made up of accusations, lies and gossip. Just check our television programs, newspapers, magazines, radio, internet, and movies. We are constantly being bombarded with stories about people cheating, lying, and accusing others of being the reason for the mess they are in. Such practices have even gotten entertainment value. Somehow watching the misery of others as a result of lying and cheating has become big business!

The Bible, however, teaches us not to accuse anyone falsely. We have to be careful what we say about each other. Is it possible to stay away from the world's attitude? Is it possible to live and speak the truth, even if the majority of people don't seem too concerned about this? How come we have wandered away from the truth? Is there a clear definition for truth?

It is one thing to say we don't speak negative or gossip or lie, but what *do* we do? Do we have a loving attitude towards others? Not gossiping doesn't make us Christians; not lying doesn't do so either. It is not by the things we don't do that we will be recognized as children of God. It is by what we do: loving God and loving others. In the previous books in this series I have clarified the fact that we are no longer asked to simply obey the Law but to fulfill it in love, just as Jesus did. Romans 13:10 (NIV) tells us that *Love does no harm to a neighbor. Therefore love is the fulfillment of the law.*

The letter of the Old Testament law says 'do not accuse anyone falsely', the Spirit says 'speak truth'. The Holy Spirit will always urge us to change from the inside out. In this book we will take a closer look at Truth, yes, with a capital T, and discover its awesome power and identity.

Marja Meijers

9th Commandment

Do not accuse anyone falsely.

Exodus 20:16

1

Nothing but the truth

Do not lie to one another, for you have put off the old self with its habits…

Colossians 3:9

Imagine a court room. A humble, quiet man has been brought in. He is being accused of a crime. No one seems to know exactly what kind of crime, even the judge doesn't know for sure. What he *does* know however, is that all kind of charges and complaints have been filed against this man. He is trying to sort things out. Justice must prevail!

During the trial several people come forward to tell lies about the defendant, who appears particularly quiet and peaceful during this ordeal. His sad but friendly eyes drift around the room only to rest for a mere second or so on some of his countrymen. They look back with hatred and spit in his direction as if to silence his kindness. It is clear that some accusers, for whatever reason, are trying to find false evidence against him. To the outsider it seems truth does not really matter, the people present in the court room just want him condemned. The angry mob grows restless and dares the judge to declare this man guilty. It does not take long before they are screaming bloody murder, 'kill him!' The louder they scream, the more serene the silence becomes that surrounds the young man. The judge starts feeling uneasy and persuades the defendant to speak up for himself. When that finally happens, the words penetrate his soul full force and startle him. Not because this man spoke with a loud voice or gave an excellent speech, but because of the depth and spiritual significance of his softly spoken testimony,

I was born and came into the world for this one purpose, to speak about the truth (John 18:37).

The judge now gets very nervous. Why in the world would people want to condemn a man who came to speak about the truth? What was the crime in doing so? Was the truth something the crowd did not want to hear?

You probably have recognized this scene. It is the historical case Truth vs. Lie and it happened some two thousand years ago when Jesus stood before Roman governor Pilate. It happened when the religious establishment accused Jesus of proclaiming to be the Son of God. Such truth was too difficult to hear and too hard to bear. As far as they were concerned the God of Israel was One, He did not have a Son equal to Himself. Claiming so would be considered blasphemy. Yes, the prophet Isaiah had spoken about a child to come, a son to be given, who would be their ruler, their Messiah. He would be called, *Wonderful Counselor, Mighty God, Eternal Father, Prince of Peace.* But that was a prophecy yet to be fulfilled for all of Israel to see and certainly not applicable to this meek and beaten-up man standing before them.

In a way I can sympathize with their initial shock as they realized this well-known rabbi went around calling God His Father. Think about it, some of them grew up around Jesus and His family. They probably ordered some furniture or tools at His father's wood shop and later on they let Him teach in their synagogues. The Scriptures confirm that He was a popular speaker and teacher and praised by everyone:

He taught in their meeting places to everyone's acclaim and pleasure (Luke 4:15 MSG).

It is one thing to be praised and popular, yet another thing to proclaim that God Himself has sent you to preach the Good News. That statement caused the religious leaders to stir and eventually explode into a jealous rage. They had a lunatic on their hands, a religious freak and extremist. They had to protect their flocks from this man, His words and deeds. After all, this Jesus called for revolution which simply meant they would be losing their audience. Somewhere down the line they had entered a religious competition and began to realize that they were failing miserably.

The Pharisees then said to one another, "You see, we are not succeeding at all! Look, the whole world is following him!" (John 12:19).

The realization that they were losing power to this young man, who refused to join in any of their religious games, was devastating. Looking back at events it is obvious that the whole case against Jesus was a fraud from the beginning.

Long before the religious leaders dragged Him before Pilate they had already plotted to kill Him, probably as a result of the jealousy I just described. They only needed to find someone who was willing to execute Him, since their law forbade them to put anyone to death (John 18:31). Besides being jealous they were also offended because Jesus broke some of their laws, for example when He healed a man on the Sabbath. They called Him to order, but Jesus explained to them that His heavenly Father was always working and that He desired to do so as well. The religious leaders were furious (John 5:18),

This saying made the Jewish authorities all the more determined to kill him; not only had he broken the Sabbath law, but he had said that God was his own Father and in this way had made himself equal with God.

This was right at the beginning of Jesus's ministry and already they were determined to kill Him. It did not even matter that they had to come up with false evidence, as long as they would succeed in silencing Him. Truth did not matter, truth had to die! When it finally came to that point, it was at that moment in history Pilate uttered one of mankind's most desperate questions ever asked until this day: and what is truth?

And what is truth? Pilate's question still lingers in our court rooms today. Pilate's question still lingers in the lives of millions of people today. Jesus before Pilate, or Truth vs. Lie, is the most important case ever presented in human history. It replays every day, for all of us, because we make choices based on what we believe to be truth. We buy, we trade, we marry, we vote, we pick, we choose and we decide based on what we consider to be the right thing to do. Yet, we silently wonder: what if I am wrong, how do I know for sure whether I have the right information, how do I know if I made the best decision? Often, if not always, the news, the facts, the stories and the promises we receive have been filtered and altered, like in Pilate's case. It was very difficult for him to make a proper decision since so many voices were trying to get through to him. Well, since then time has passed and history has been written but things have not changed much.

Today we are constantly being bombarded with voices and opinions. Books, television, newspapers, movies, the internet, they are all fighting to get our attention and our vote! We live in the information age and everything and everyone around us is urging us to buy into their message, product or opinion. We watch, read, and listen and try to find our way among the images, voices and headlines that are frantically trying to penetrate our minds and rule our lives, each one of them claiming to be real and truthful.

The result is a-kind-of-truth that varies with the seasons and fads and can be very confusing. Truth has become rather vague in our society. It is no longer a solid rock we can stand on. Truth has been made into a variable belief. For example, at one time we learned that milk was good for us and we really believed that. A few years later, in the name of science, dairy had to be avoided to stay healthy and again many people believed that. It is possible that a few years from now, after much research and as a result of new developments, dairy will become an essential ingredient of a healthy diet again. Now, what is true? This is only a very simple example and one of thousands passing by each day. We consider something to be true based on what others are saying about it. In case of doubt we just follow our intuition: if it feels good, it must be good and it could be true.

So, along the way we have made up our own truths which we use for personal advantage, for example to sell a product or idea, to justify behavior or to make something sound good. We say things like 'everyone is doing it, it cannot be bad', 'there is no law against it, so we can try' and 'it works for me, why don't you try it?' And so we participate in making truth even more indefinite and variable. But deep down inside I believe we can probably all relate to Pilate's desperate question 'and what is truth?' It is the basic question behind every decision we make and if truth varies from day to day our decisions are nothing more than reactions to instinct and responses to feelings. Friends today, enemies tomorrow, happily married this year, bitterly divorced next year. We find ourselves going up and down with the flow of the season and fashion trends and needless to say this makes us very restless. No solid ground to stand on, no anchor to hold on to. This unrest hovers over society today and results in much unbalance. I can see this around me wherever I go. People being uncertain about their education, their future, their marriage, their identity, even their faith.

I believe a society will be sent into free fall when it decides to let go of God's moral standards. It might look liberating and exciting at first, until it hits the pavement of course. No matter how much independence, liberty and sometimes total anarchy are being promoted, more people than ever before are desperately crying out for truth, for a stabilizing factor in an ever changing troubled world. Truth would ease our worries, heal our pain and bring balance and peace in our frantic lives. That is why I would like to take Truth with a capital T as the foundation for this book, as it is the answer to a world that is in desperate need of direction. It is also the practical implementation of the 9th Commandment.

At first I thought that writing about the 9th Commandment as given in Exodus 20:16, *'do not accuse anyone falsely'*, would be an easy job. The book would have the size of a refrigerator magnet. I imagined it to go like this: 'Hey folks, don't lie, okay?' Wouldn't that be a great campaign in the quest for truth? I could give orders to manufacture a million pieces and distribute them in schools, churches, supermarkets, movie theaters and businesses. Great idea and it could work for some people. Nevertheless, I doubt if such a campaign would have a positive outcome in general, because telling people what *not* to do will create either rebellious or passive individuals. On one hand people who are resisting God because they see him as the God who only tells them what they cannot do. On the other hand people who are inactive because they are so afraid to make a mistake. No, the refrigerator magnet idea is the wrong way of tackling this topic. Simply because in this book series it is no longer about what we *don't* do, but rather about what we *can* do! Instead of focusing on what the Law tells us not to do, we want to focus on what the Holy

Spirit desires to do through us. In other words, we will have to practically apply the spiritual principle behind the 9th Commandment in our present day time and thinking.

Let me clarify this. The 9th Commandment says *'do not accuse anyone falsely'*. Now, it would be very hard to go around all day focusing on the fact that we are not supposed to say anything false against anyone. That would be a frustrating way to live. Let's face it, it is not good to focus on negative statements. It would be the same as going around all day, saying 'I cannot smoke' or 'I cannot have cookies'. Focusing on what we cannot do will have the opposite effect; it will activate our craving, simply because we put all our attention to it. Anyone who has ever tried to quit bad habits that way knows how difficult and frustrating it can be. In this book series we therefore want to focus on the positive, the things we *can* do to please God! The Bible says in Ephesians 5:10,

Try to learn what pleases the Lord.

It takes time and effort to learn more about God and the kind of life we can live to please Him. Isn't the same thing true for our relationships and friendships? We must spend time together, do things together, talk, listen, and ask questions if we want to get to know our friend, spouse or neighbor any better. It takes time and effort to build healthy relationships. How much more effort should we make to work on our relationship with God.

Now, we do not have to win His love; God LOVES us! But from a Biblical point of view it is good to learn what pleases Him.

I believe the Bible has the answers to the issues we are dealing with from day to day. It is not the boring and old fashioned book some people think it is. It is the book of truth and we need to dust it off. Let us shift our focus. Let us look at God's Word from a different perspective, the perspective Jesus shows us. He was a rabbi, He knew the Law. Yet, He was full of grace and truth,

The Word became a human being and, full of grace and truth, lived among us (John 1:14a)

Meditate on the following:

- *How do I make my everyday choices? Are they based on impulse, feelings, other people's opinion or something else?*
- *What is my definition of truth?*
- *Do I seek to please God? If yes, how?*

Journal your thoughts:

2

Love and Law

For the entire law is fulfilled in keeping this one command: "Love your neighbor as yourself."

Galatians 5:14 (NIV)

Whether growing up in a Christian family or not, most people have a certain perspective on Christianity, God and the Bible. We see everything through the glasses of our upbringing, church denomination, books read, education received and experiences shared.

Jesus showed the people of His time how to change their perception of God's Word, which had been handed down over the centuries. In the fifth chapter of Matthew's gospel Jesus says over and over 'You have heard that it was said' and following that He quotes the Law. People must have been nodding their heads; they knew what the Law said. Jesus then urges the people to think about their behavior up until that moment and continues with the following words: 'but now I tell you'. He then gives them the upside down, inside out, radical version of the Law, the new law of love. This law of love is sometimes called the law of Christ, for example in Galatians 6:2,

Help carry one another's burdens, and in this way you will obey the law of Christ.

I would like to emphasize that Jesus did not say the Law as they knew it was no longer there. I believe He showed them a new way of looking at it.

Jesus told the crowds, who had gathered around Him on that day, that the commandment not to commit adultery really should take root in a person's heart. He told them that whoever even looked after a woman with lust would be guilty of committing adultery. Well, that made most men present guilty of breaking this law! And that was exactly the point Jesus wanted to make. We are all guilty, so we all need a Savior. When He addressed the crowds that day, He showed them that obedience to God was no longer a matter of keeping certain written laws but a matter of a changed heart. His way of explaining things blew people away! Matthew 7:28 tells us,

When Jesus finished saying these things, the crowd was amazed at the way he taught.

We can still be amazed by His teaching today! Maybe you always thought that the Ten Commandments were old fashioned and outdated, which really is an incorrect observation because how can the Word of God lose its power? His Word is alive and always accurate. It has no expiration date!

Of course the coming of Jesus Christ to this earth changed several really important things. When He died on the cross and was raised from the dead for the forgiveness of our sins and the healing of our diseases, the testament (the will) was opened and a new covenant, as foretold by the prophets, was announced. ALL people became heirs to the promise, not just the Jewish people. That is in a nutshell the good news. The Torah (teaching) was being fulfilled in the life of Jesus. Was that the end of the Old Testament? Has the New Testament replaced the Old Testament? Can we rip it out of our Bibles today? No, of course not! All Scripture has been given for our benefit. For example, we can learn a lot about God's character by studying His dealings with the Israelites. We can learn much about the history of the Middle East by reading the Old Testament. We can discover the Jewish roots of the Christian faith in the ancient writings, and so on, and so on.

With this in mind Jesus not only urged the people of His time to fulfill the old teachings, He still urges every believer today to do so. It is an ongoing thing. We are called to bring life to the written Word by practicing it. We are called to be doers of the Word, not hearers (or readers for that matter) only. How? In Matthew 7:12 Jesus explains this new way of implementing the Law in our daily lives quite simply as follows,

Do for others what you want them to do for you: this is the meaning of the Law of Moses and of the teachings of the prophets.

Now that is a totally different approach than the one religious leaders and devoted believers have taken on for centuries: telling other people what they can or cannot do. This approach says that we should treat others the way we want to be treated because *that* is the meaning of the Law! *That* is the true meaning of the Ten Commandments. Maybe you have never looked at them from Jesus's point of view. Often we still envision them as the two stone tablets Moses received, which of course is a wonderful picture. However, after God wrote the Ten Commandments on stone tablets with His finger, the people violated them every day. It did not come naturally to obey.

Today the Law is no longer written on stone tablets, it is written in the heart of every believer,

This is the covenant that I will make with them in the days to come, says the Lord: I will put my laws in their hearts and write them on their minds (Hebrews 10:16).

That is a wonderful promise, God's laws in our hearts and on our minds. His laws are in us, are part of our being. Yet, when we take a realistic look into our lives we will see that it does not come naturally to live according to what He has put in us, according to this new nature. It should come naturally maybe, but the fact of the matter is, it doesn't. Just take an honest look at your own life and the world around you. Are we living in perfect harmony with God's will? Are we automatically obeying His Word whenever we think, talk or act? No, we still need guidance. The Holy Spirit and God's Word are there to teach us. Many people today believe that once they have received God's grace and love, life will be good forevermore. The Bible, however, clearly teaches a transformation process which begins with a single step. I am a witness of this transformation process in my own life but also in the lives of many men and women we encounter during our travels.

My husband and I are the founders of a non-profit organization that supports and encourages rehabilitation programs all over Europe and the Middle East. These programs accept men and women who have life controlling problems such as alcohol and drugs addictions. Sometimes they have lived on the streets or in prison for many years. When they surrender their lives to Jesus Christ they become new creations. This is truly the biggest miracle any person can experience and we never grow tired of listening to their testimonies. Now, why does an ex-addict need months and months of teaching and training to renew his or her mind? Well, because even though their spirit has been renewed, their soul is still the same with all the hurts, habits and hang-ups from the old life. It takes time to heal, to restore, to forgive, to accept and to love oneself. Of course this transformation and sanctification process is not only needed when you have been an addict, homeless or criminal. It applies to all of us no matter where we are coming from. Every person has a story to tell and scars that need healing. In Colossians 3:9-10 the Apostle Paul explains that this life according to a new nature is an ongoing process,

Do not lie to one another, for you have put off the old self with its habits and have put on the new self. This is the new being which God, its Creator, is constantly renewing in his own image, in order to bring you to a full knowledge of himself.

We must purposely take *off* the old self and put *on* the new self. It does not come automatically because we believe in Jesus, although He is the one constantly renewing us in His own image. Yes, spiritually speaking we are a new being, a new creation through God's grace. But naturally speaking, when it comes to 'self', we need to take off the old and put on the new whether we are an ex-addict or not. This goes for everyone.

According to Paul's words in the Scripture mentioned above, taking off the old self means we stop lying to one another (don't do this) and it should be followed by putting on the new self, which means we speak the truth (rather do this)… which is exactly the theme of this book. I know this book will help to bring things in a proper perspective, relevant to the time we live in now, without doing away with a single Scripture.

This is already the sixth book in the Ten Commandments Series. The previous books discussed a wide variety of topics: our 24/7 society, family life, money matters, sinful desires and even abortion. By placing the commandments right in the middle of our daily lives in the 21st century, they make a lot more sense than the picture of the stone tablets or the printed version in old languages. We deal with these issues every day! The key is to look at the old teachings with the knowledge and understanding we have now. We need fresh insights on ancient truths. The apostle Paul understood it like no one else. He was a scholar, a teacher of the Law, a Pharisee. I feel free to say he knew the Law but he also knew grace like no other. He experienced it firsthand when he fell to the ground on his way to Damascus and met Jesus who asked why he persecuted Him. In his zeal Paul had fanatically persecuted the followers of Jesus, the people of the Way. The new way of love... But God showed him grace. In his letter to the Romans Paul comes to the point where he writes,

Be under no obligation to no one-the only obligation you have is to love one another. Whoever does this has obeyed the Law (Romans 13:8).

Well, he summed it up in one sentence. Love is the answer to all requirements of the Law. Love for God and love for our neighbor. He goes on (verse 10) and writes a statement that I have used as the basis for this book series:

If you love someone, you will never do him wrong; to love, then, is to obey the whole Law.

Or, as it says in other translations: love is the fulfillment of the Law. We will take a closer look at this statement in the next chapter. What matters at this moment is that we value God's Word as a whole, that we are willing to take a fresh look at His commandments and that we expect to learn more about Him. God does not regret, change or delete sections of His Word and we should not do so either. I dare you to take a fresh look at the old teachings and see for yourself whether the words come alive or not.

In this book we will see that The New Testament takes the 9th Commandment a level up, as we can read in Ephesians 4:25 (NIV),

Therefore each of you must put off falsehood and speak truthfully to his neighbor…

Now, there you have it! This is exactly the law of Christ, the new way of love. It is one thing to say we will never accuse anyone falsely, but that is simply keeping or obeying the Law. We must take it a step up if we want to fulfill (or implement) the Law in love. It is no longer about what we cannot or should not do, but about what God's Spirit wants to do through us. Instead of refraining from false accusations we must learn to speak truthfully. That is the next level, the new way of the Spirit.

We have to learn to look at Gods commandments on a different level. Instead of seeing them as just a bunch of rules that are hard to obey, we should be eager to see them in light of our transformation into the likeness of Jesus. Instead of saying 'well, it seems I better keep my mouth shut' for fear that something unwholesome wants to come out, we should be open to learn how to be filled with truth. Speaking truthfully must become our new nature, the result and fruit of our transformation. Living that way has nothing to do with just obeying a set of rules. Living that way is following the desire of our heart to please God.

Before we take a closer look into this Truth vs. Lie case, let us start with a little exercise to get our minds working on this topic. Try to define *Truth* in a few words. Get a piece of paper and write it down. Let your mind and heart work and think seriously about the following questions. What is truth for me personally? Where do I find it, do I see it presented in something or someone? Is it a definition, a statement, a lifestyle, a matter of conscience or merely the opposite of falsehood? Where do I get my sense of truth from? Do I always speak the truth? What I am really getting at is: are we able to answer Pilate's question?

Keep these thoughts nearby and check them again after reading this book. I dare you to find out if your 'truth' is still the same.

Meditate on the following:

- ❖ *What are my thoughts on the Ten Commandments?*
- ❖ *To love is to obey the whole Law. How can I make this practical?*
- ❖ *How do I decide whether what someone says is true?*

Journal your thoughts:

3

Between rules and freedom

If you obey my teaching, you are really my disciples; you will know the truth, and the truth will set you free.

John 8:31-32

Before writing another word about the 9th Commandment I want to make sure that I mention, as I have done in all previous books, that the only way to stand right before almighty God is through His grace and our faith in His Son Jesus Christ.

We can never do anything to deserve a healthy relationship and eternal life with God, it is a gift. A gift cannot be earned, only be given and received! A healthy relationship with our Creator is based on His grace and our faith and should never be driven by shame, guilt or religion. Obeying the commandments will not necessarily bring us closer to God and will certainly not give us eternal life; only faith in Jesus can do that. Not even speaking the truth at all times would be enough to gain access to God. Jesus Christ is the only way to the heavenly Father. Jesus explained this clearly in John 14:6 (NIV),

I am the way, the truth, and the life; no one comes to the Father except through me.

This does not leave us much choice. Yes, I know people have tried and are still trying to find other ways to connect with God but the Bible makes it clear; there is no other way! I realize this may be offensive as well as disappointing to many people who are trying to find their own convenient way to connect with the God of the Universe.

But let's keep it simple; we can hug a tree, wear precious stones around our neck, try to seek our inner self through meditation or practice any other religious ritual, it will not bring us into an intimate relationship with God. These practices might briefly produce a good feeling or bring some form of enlightenment, but they will never, ever answer our life's questions and will certainly not lead to the forgiveness of sins. Now, you might ask, if only faith in Jesus and His offer of forgiveness can give us access to God, why study the Ten Commandments then? What does that add to a relationship with God? Well, Jesus spoke intensively about the Law and by listening to Him we will learn from Him. Jesus says that loving God and loving others is the meaning of the Law and the prophets. Therefore, a life of love is the implementation of the commandments. Living a better and more godly life here on earth will spread His love and build a better society. All these things are pleasing to

God. He loves this earth and He loves the people that inhabit it. It is God's desire that we actually enjoy our lives and live in harmony with Him and each other! This is the way of love. It begins with God loving us first (grace) and with us answering His love (faith) by believing in our heart and confessing with our mouth that Jesus is Lord (Romans 10:9-10),

If you confess that Jesus is Lord and believe that God raised him from death, you will be saved. For it is by our faith that we are put right with God; it is by our confession that we are saved.

I am a product of God's love and grace and I see it as a huge privilege to write with passion and enthusiasm about His Law (Torah or teaching) in this book series. It is my prayer that the Holy Spirit, through my writing, will set you totally free from preconceived ideas, wrong doctrine and distorted views of the Bible. So many Christians struggle with finding a healthy balance between reading the Old and New Testament, between law and grace, between rules and freedom, which often results in very extreme ideas and interpretations. It is my goal to bring a healthy and balanced message that will increase the joy in the life of every believer and glorify God.

I certainly realize it is not easy to write about God's Law, about the Ten Commandments, from a fresh perspective in a time and age where grace has been exalted over everything else, even over God's own Word. A popular one-liner which can be heard in many homes, churches and teachings is: 'It is all grace!' Well, if it is *all* grace, what do we need faith for? Or love or truth for that matter? If it is all grace there is nothing more to learn, there is no sanctification, no growth, no suffering, no obedience. Don't get me wrong, God's grace has been poured out on this world and God's grace is available to every person on earth. Hallelujah! But we have to answer His love call with faith in His Son and obedience to His teachings. Without faith we cannot even please God. There are two sides to every coin. Grace is wonderful, but it does not move mountains. Faith is powerful, but without love it is useless. Truth is essential, but it needs to be balanced with wisdom. Love never fails, yet it hurts at times. We must be careful not to separate these from each other. They are all part of God's character and thus fruit that His Holy Spirit will produce in us. So, I pray you will be able to read this book series with an open and receptive heart and a sincere love for God's Word.

I have based this series on several important scriptures. First of all on the words of Jesus in Matthew 5:17 where He was teaching about the Law and said,

Do not think that I have come to do away with the Law of Moses and the teachings of the prophets. I have not come

to do away with them, but to make their teachings come true.

Now, if Jesus did not come to do away with the Law, why would we think we could? We would be contradicting His words. As followers of Jesus we are asked to do the same: make the teachings come true. Some translations say that Jesus came to fulfill the Law. That didn't happen just once, that is still happening today through us! Every time we make the teachings come true, we fulfill the Law, just like Jesus did and He is our ultimate example.

How then do we fulfill or implement the Law? This brings us to the second scripture I have based my writings on: Romans 13:10,

Love is the fulfillment of the Law.

Was Jesus the only one who ever loved? No, He urges us to do the same. Every time we act in love, we fulfill the Law. We make the teachings come true. This is a repeating action. Jesus has set the example. We follow. Love is a matter of the heart, not of rules and regulations. This series is not about keeping or obeying the Law, it is all about the implementation in our daily lives. It is all about the way of love. Many Christians claim that we, as sinful human beings, cannot fulfill the Law as Jesus did, who knew no sin. By saying such a thing we are basically saying we are unable to love.

Love therefore is the answer. Not human love, but love that comes from God. The kind of love that the Holy Spirit wants to produce in us and through us,

But the fruit of the Spirit is love, joy, peace, patience, kindness, goodness, faithfulness, gentleness and self-control. Against such things there is no law (Galatians 5:22, NIV).

This godly love overrules the Law. If love is the answer, why is it then we still hurt each other? Why is it then we are living in a world full of lies, in a country where people get accused in court, in church, in the media and even within their own family circles? The air is filled with charges (false or not) against our fellow men. Was I ignorant when I thought 'finally a simple topic' when I read the 9th Commandment? Does it not all come down to this: God wants us to speak the truth? If everyone would just stop blaming others for their trouble and simply tell the truth when asked, we would be living in a better world. We could actually love each other.

Well, that might be my wishful thinking but it certainly does not reflect reality. Now you might say: I never accused anyone falsely, I would never do that. But then again, this book is not so much about what we don't do, but about what we can and should do! Obedience to the Law is the way of the Old Testament, fulfillment of the Law is the new way of the Spirit. The apostle Paul explains extensively in chapter eight in the letter to the Romans what that new way of the Spirit is; it is a life controlled by God's Holy Spirit, no longer by our own ego. In verse six he says,

To be controlled by the Spirit results in life and peace.

Isn't that what we are all looking for, life and peace? That is the firm balance missing in our world today: true life and real peace. The Bible says we can have it if we let the Spirit control us. If we are able to let the Spirit control what we think, say or do, we will enter that life and have peace. The Holy Spirit lives in every person who believes in his heart and confesses with his mouth that Jesus is Lord. Go ahead, do it, say it, believe it! It is surely possible to know and to live the truth.

That brings us to the third scripture I based this book series on. You can find it in Romans 7:6,

No longer do we serve in the old way of a written law, but in the new way of the Spirit.

What is this new way of the Spirit? It simply means that we should no longer live according to our human nature, but according to what the Spirit wants. And the Spirit of God is love and produces divine (unconditional) love in us. Romans 5:5 (NIV) says,

...God's love has been poured out into our hearts through the Holy Spirit, who has been given to us.

We have to learn to see God's commandments from a loving perspective. Many people see God's commandments as strict rules that will limit their freedom and not as loving guidelines from a parent to a child. God set them up for our well-being! He is concerned with the way we live our lives. He is concerned with our well-being, with the condition of our hearts and souls.

Throughout the Old and New Testament God gives His people advice for the development of vocational, relational and social skills. When God gave the Ten Commandments to Moses, He later on explained them in detail to him. He did not send Moses down the mountain with just a little not-to-do list; He talked with him for a length of time and instructed him carefully. He explained the various moral and religious laws, the laws of holiness, justice and fairness. He didn't just say: be good. He knew Moses would ask Him: 'but, what is good?' Having knowledge about His laws is not enough, we need understanding. As I said before, they will not bring us eternal life, but they will bring us a better life here on earth and we should be interested in that plan as long as we are here.

With the new way of the Spirit in mind, let us look at the NIV translation of the 9th Commandment. It says,

You shall not give false testimony against your neighbor.

Very plainly put, the 9th Commandment tells us not to lie; not to our neighbor, not about our neighbor. The Hebrew word neighbor here is not just the person who literally lives next door, but *a friend, associate, countrymen or another person.*

When we read words like 'testimony' or 'accusation', it is important to think beyond the courtroom. We need to make it personal for our own lives. Every time we say something about someone that is not true, we are falsely accusing that person and we are lying about that person. It often starts with simple things we say, like 'she started it' or 'he told me it was okay' or 'she is so stupid'. Those statements might seem harmless in a conversation, but they set the stage for more accusations, bigger lies and endless debate. Proverbs 12:17 (NIV) says,

A truthful witness gives honest testimony, but a false witness tells lies.

I feel free to say that a false accusation or a false testimony is simply a lie, also outside the courtroom. My idea of a refrigerator magnet as described in chapter one wasn't so bad after all, yet it misses the point. If we cannot lie, we will have to speak the truth at all times, right? How do we get to the point where it is always the truth that we speak? Let's face it, we live right in the middle of a world in which uttering false accusations and lies is common practice and it is difficult to stand up against it by not participating, by actually wanting to do the opposite: speaking the truth.

I grew up in culture where it is not common practice to file lawsuits and it is shocking for me to see how in the USA for example, sane and even educated human beings are trying to destroy each other by telling lies, spreading gossip and filing lawsuits in court. I am not saying that all charges are false, but many of them are. I believe that often the main goal is to find a scapegoat, to create a case and a public spectacle, *not* a quest for truth or justice. What has happened to the minds of people who file (false) accusations against fellow humans or businesses? What has happened to a society which somehow turned lying, gossiping and blaming into entertainment? Why do we love to engage in these practices?

Maybe personally you have never accused anyone falsely, but I believe that by reading gossip and by watching certain television shows we are participating in the atmosphere of accusation that is hovering over our country. By feeding ourselves with public allegations we store up bad things in our hearts and the next time we speak up something equally bad will come out.

Maybe you think I am taking this way too seriously. A little lie here and there, a juicy lawsuit, a little tasty gossip; that won't ruin the world. Well, it *does* ruin the world as God wants it to be and as Christians we certainly cannot engage in it because if we feed on bad things, we will grow on bad things and we will eventually produce bad things.

Now, you might say again: I never accused anyone falsely, I would never do that. But then, this book is not so much about what we don't do, but about what we can and should do. Remember this! When God gave the 9th Commandment to His people He made it plain and simple: do not accuse anyone falsely. Other translations say: do not lie or cheat or do not give false testimony. It all comes down to the fact that God wants us to speak the truth whenever we open our mouths. The question remains, why doesn't it come naturally for us to speak truthfully? Let us take a closer and in-depth look at the age old battle between truth and lies.

Meditate on the following:

❖ *Do I have the tendency to blame others for my mistakes?*

❖ *What is my definition of gossip? Do I engage in it?*

❖ *Do I recall a situation where truth was painful? And equally: when was a lie painful?*

Journal your thoughts:

4

History of deception

Truth stumbles in the public square, and honesty finds no place there

Isaiah 59:14

In order to gain some understanding about the battle between truth and falsehood we do have to go way back in history. We have to go back to the Garden of Eden where truth was opposed and the root of all falsehood became visible: deception.

The fact of the matter is that truth has been twisted in many ways ever since the events in the Garden of Eden. We can look back at thousands of years of human history saturated with deception (twisted truth). Beginning with Adam and Eve, our history has been filled with distorted truth and people pointing fingers, judging, condemning and blaming others. And let's face it: this is still one of the ways we are making history. When something goes terribly wrong in a nation, city, street, school, church or family, the first thing we often do is look for someone to blame. Pointing fingers, or 'the blame game' as one of my pastors calls it, has become a survival mechanism for many people from all walks of life. It keeps us from taking full responsibility for our own words and deeds and it can keep us in a victim role for the longest time. It is easy to blame someone else for things gone wrong, but we have to learn to look at our own actions first.

As I wrote earlier, accusing others falsely has gotten high entertainment value. We find people lying, cheating, gossiping and accusing whenever we turn on the television or open a magazine. Just take a look at the magazine stand in your store or maybe even at the reading material on your coffee table. It seems we haven't moved up the ladder of integrity very much since Adam and Eve. We say things we don't really want to say, often we don't think before we talk and sad but true, it is not always the truth we are speaking. We can engage in slander or gossip without realizing we are falsely accusing people. Who can tell a lie from the truth? I believe it is time to reconsider Pilate's question.

According to the Bible the existence of humanity started off pretty awesome, but it changed drastically. That altered atmosphere has set the stage for an ongoing battle between good and evil, or truth versus lies. From the very first beginning of human history there has been deception, let's say trickery or fraud, which is the root of all falsehood. We will have to go back to Genesis 3 where we can read how it all started. The scenario is probably familiar to most people. There is peace and truth in the Garden of Eden, life is a beach, then one day a terrible thing happened. Adam and Eve disobeyed God and as a result their relationship with Him became distorted. Sin became the barrier for a healthy relationship between God and men. When God asked about their motives for disobeying Him, both Adam and Eve had the same kind of answer: I didn't do it. In other words, it wasn't my fault and to prove their point they blamed someone else and so did the snake.

The snake tried to make God a liar by denying what He had said (verse 4), Adam told God that Eve made him do it (verse 12) and Eve blamed the snake for tricking her (verse 13). By basically calling God a liar the devil started off his business of deception and accusation on earth and he has been engaged in it ever since. I must admit he did a tricky job with Eve. I mean, my response would probably have been the same. Take a closer look at the familiar scene and find out for yourself how easy it is to be deceived.

God had put two special trees in the Garden of Eden (Genesis 2:9): the tree that gives life and the tree that gives knowledge of good and bad. He told Adam (not Eve by the way, because she simply was not created yet) not to eat from the tree that gives knowledge of good and bad,

You may eat the fruit of any tree in the garden, except the tree that gives knowledge of what is good and what is bad. You must not eat the fruit of that tree; if you do, you will die the same day (Genesis 2:16-17).

This tells me Adam was allowed to eat from the other special tree, the tree of life. Later, Eve came on the scene and she had an encounter with the snake who personified evil. The snake was shrewd when he picked his battle with Eve. He could have gone to Adam, but obviously it was easier to deceive Eve because she got the information about the forbidden tree second hand! She told the snake what she had heard from Adam, namely that they were not allowed to eat from the tree of knowledge of good and bad because it would result in death. The devil confused her when he said 'you will not die, you will just know all about good and bad'. She figured he was right, since the tree was called the tree of knowledge of good and bad.

It is my guess that her reasoning went somewhat like this: 'eating from the tree of life is allowed and prevents us from dying. So how can we possibly die if we eat from the tree of knowledge of good and bad? That has nothing to do with living or dying.' She probably thought that if they would eat from the wisdom tree they would become wise and still live forever because they could still eat from the tree of life. It was a tricky situation and she fell for the snake's cunning way of deceiving her. Be honest, wouldn't you have been tempted to become wise and live forever?

Of course God is not a liar, the devil is! He is a liar and the father of all lies (John 8:44). When Adam and Eve ate from the tree of knowledge of good and bad they did indeed become wise; the snake was right when he said that. Genesis 3:22 tells us

Then the Lord God said, now the man has become like one of us and has knowledge of what is good and what is bad.

God no longer allowed them to eat from the other tree, the tree of life, and so that became the second forbidden tree. Adam and Eve's decision to eat from the first forbidden tree was basically the end of their eternal life on earth, they became mortal men. They had signed their spiritual death sentence; the snake lied when he said that that could never happen.

Ever since the devil accused God of being a liar; that deception has been hovering over the world. In the Garden of Eden everyone somehow accused someone else for their mistakes; today many people still have that same attitude. We just learned that mankind does have knowledge about what is good and bad or let's say what is true and what is a lie. At first Adam and Eve did not know anything about good and bad, that knowledge was hidden in the fruit of the tree and they could not eat from it. They basically enjoyed eternal live with God, which was of course just fine. Maybe the sole reason they fell for the trick of the snake was the fact that they could not detect good or bad, all they had was a free will to choose. The whole episode with the snake did cost them their lives; God did no longer allow them to live forever on earth. But at the same time He allowed them to keep their free will, the will to choose between the truth and a lie.

Now, if humanity gained wisdom, how come it kept falling and is still falling for the lies of the devil? The key word here is deception! When the devil saw the success he had by simply twisting the truth, he was on a roll! If he could stop people from seeing truth, from speaking truth and ultimately from acting in truth, he would always be able to stand between God and them. If he could do this once, he could do it again and again and so began his quest to destroy the truth. And sadly it is still quite easy for him to twist truth and make it sound okay. We all know examples of this, I am sure. It happens when we 'lie' on our tax return or state a lower sales price at the DMV for a car we just bought. It happens when we allow other people to talk us into something we know isn't right.

The bad news is that deception came into the world through Satan. We just saw how he cleverly started his game and he has been pretty successful ever since. The good news is that truth came into the world through Jesus Christ. John 1:17 states that,

God gave the Law through Moses, but grace and truth came through Jesus Christ.

Truth came into the world in the form of a human being from divine descent. Now that must have been a bad day for the enemy, for he had been running rampant for centuries. According to the gospel of Matthew, king Herod wanted to kill Jesus, who came to talk about the truth, while He was still a baby. He mass murdered all the little boys at that time just to make sure this Jesus would not survive. However hard he tried, he did not succeed. John 1:14 tells us that,

The Word became a human being and, full of grace and truth, lived among us.

Jesus was full of truth and He lived among the people of His time. He was on a quest too, as He told Pilate. He came to speak about the truth and He did so in His own court case. He upheld or fulfilled the 9th Commandment right there and then. The words Jesus spoke before Pilate (John 18:37) seem to be off track, even strange,

Whoever belongs to the truth listens to me.

In the midst of lies and accusations He spoke about the truth. His answer came before Pilate even asked the question. Jesus told him: 'listen to Me!' If we want to learn more about the truth, we have to listen to Him indeed!

Jesus did many good deeds while He was on earth. Even those who did not believe that He was the Son of God agreed that He was a charitable person, a good man. Yet, the religious establishment as well as the common people hurled false accusations at Him, even long before He stood in front of Pilate! Jesus asked about their motives in John 10:32,

I have done many good deeds in your presence which the Father gave me to do; for which one of these do you want to stone me?

He came to do good deeds, He came to talk about the truth, yet the people wanted to kill Him. His teaching was too hard to bear for many people of His time, it was the reason for a lot of turmoil and it was the reason for His death sentence. Jesus told Pilate that His purpose on earth was to speak about the truth. Pilate wondered out loud: 'and what is truth?'

The more I studied this scripture in John 18:37-38, the more Pilate's question started to bother me. It is such a desperate cry for help. Pilate was surrounded by lies and false accusations and the screaming masses blurred his thinking and vision. This happened despite the fact that his wife warned him that Jesus was innocent and that she had suffered much about Him in a dream. Pilate was not able to stand up for truth and he almost begged Jesus to give the answer for him. I asked myself 'am I able to answer Pilate's question in a manner that will still help people today?' I knew it wouldn't be enough to write a book on how to avoid false accusations or about the devastating results of engaging in lies or to manufacture a few thousand refrigerator magnets for that matter. It had to be a book about Truth, with a capital 'T', sort of an apologetic work for the common folk, like you and me.

I am the kind of person that is always reading a few books at the same time. In our house there are books in every room, on the night stands, in the family room and stacks and stacks on every possible table or dresser. I might read a novel, a non-fiction book and an apologetic work at the same time. Some books intrigue me; they stay with me even after putting them down. I simply don't want them to end and my reading slows down while flipping through the pages. Some books ask for a second reading and lots of thinking, those are the ones I really like. The Bible is a book like that. No matter how many times I pick it up, it will always show me something new and interesting. Yet, sometimes I wonder, do I really understand the true meaning behind the words? What does it tell me about God? I do not simply want to gain knowledge or to gather information. I desire to know God better.

Let us face it. It is not too hard to do a study on the 9th Commandment for example. We can do a word search on 'false' and 'accusation' and check scriptures in the Old and New Testament regarding this subject. We will learn that speaking the truth will bless us as well as the people around us. Speaking the truth will actually keep us safe from destruction and drama. We should therefore make the decision to make it a habit to speak carefully. However, such a Bible study should not end there. Things might work that easy if we were among the only people in the world, if there was no enemy and no one to push our buttons. In reality we have to deal with challenging people and circumstances every day. Outside influences are always at work in our lives and, as the Bible states in Ephesians 6, we are in a spiritual battle, whether we like it or not. No matter how close we are to Jesus, how wonderful our relationship with Him is; the battle is raging on. I am writing this as a reality check, not as a discouraging note

Think about the apostle Peter, he was a very close and loved companion of Jesus and for several years spent time with Him every single day! Yet he could not stand under pressure, he could not tell the truth when asked. He was not able to answer Pilate's question. Deception held him captive as we will see in the next chapter.

Meditate on the following:

- *Have I ever knowingly twisted truth to suit my purposes?*

- *Do I have a tendency to talk people into doing or believing certain things?*

- *Am I willing to listen to what the Bible wants to teach me?*

Journal your thoughts:

5

Standing up for truth

Yet you are trying to kill me, because you will not accept my teaching

John 8:37

I hope by now it makes sense that the commandment 'do not accuse anyone falsely' in the new way of the Spirit would mean 'always speak the truth'. When Jesus walked the earth about two thousand years ago He was full of truth and whenever He opened His mouth, truth came out.

Wouldn't it be nice to say that this is the case when we, His followers, open our mouths? Well, this is obviously not so. Even the apostle Peter did not speak truth when it mattered most, although He had been feeding on the words and teachings of Jesus for several years. I am actually glad his failure to stand up for truth is recorded in the Bible, because it will help us in case we experience something likewise in our own lives. Even though we might feed ourselves on the Word, it is no guarantee that truth comes over our lips whenever we speak. This is because we were also fed with lots of error or un-truth in the past. Even if we speak words that sound right or are so called 'politically correct', it doesn't necessarily mean those words are right from a biblical point of view. Take a topic as global warming for example. Much has been said and written in regards to the changing of our climate. We listen to statements, we read articles in the newspaper, we might enjoy a debate etc. etc. It does not take long before we repeat what we have heard and so we take part in the enemy's strategy to sow fear on earth and to undermine biblical truth. Does God's Word have to say something about our climate? Of course! In Genesis 8:22 God speaks,

As long as the world exists, there will be a time for planting and a time for harvest. There will always be cold and heat, summer and winter, day and night.

Personally, this is my view on 'global warming'. I am not saying that we should not take proper care of our planet, but I am convinced we do not need to worry about the weather and seasons.

We have to be careful what we listen to, because it will take root in our heart. If we keep feeding ourselves with error we allow deception to take root in our heart. We have seen that deception is a strong enemy of truth; the confusing and diluting effect on our thinking works most of the time. Deception is twisted truth and it can slowly but surely creep into any circumstance or situation. It is often fed by voices, lots of voices all crying for attention. The one who speaks the loudest often gets the vote. Truth must have a permanent and prominent place in our lives in order to reveal deception. Years ago someone explained this to me using the following example: employees at a bank recognize false bank notes *not* by studying false bank notes, but by studying the real stuff. By handling thousands and thousands of legitimate bank notes they are able to recognize a false one immediately. In the same way we must not spend our time studying the tricks of the enemy. On the contrary, we must spend time with truth in order to be able to discern anything false. We will get to that in the following chapters.

For now, let us go back to Pilate one more time. Pilate played such an important role in Jesus' trial. He was the governor of Judea, he had the authority to set Jesus free or have Him crucified (John 19:10). In a way Pilate has been blamed for Jesus's death sentence. Personally I think he was more concerned about the truth than Peter at that moment. When reading through the account of the events leading up to the crucifixion of Jesus we notice that Pilate declared Jesus innocent, three times in a row, while at the same time Peter denied Jesus three times. Pilate told the truth when he said 'I cannot find any reason to condemn this man'. Peter was saying: 'I don't know this man, I've never seen Him'. Pilate was looking for a way to set Jesus free (John 19:12) while Peter was looking for a way to save his own body. Pilate knew he had truth standing right in front of him the day they met, he believed Him. Peter had been living with the truth for three years, yet he denied their relationship when it mattered most. Pilate's wife lost sleep over Jesus's trial (Matthew 27:19), the Bible says she suffered over Him, while Peter was only concerned with a place by the fire to warm himself in the cold night.

Whichever way you look at the situation, Pilate must have known the truth deep down in his heart and he was not afraid to proclaim his findings, as we can read in John 18:38,

I cannot find any reason to condemn this man.

He tried to get some answers, some confirmation from Jesus. When Jesus kept silent, the voices of deception got louder. The crowd screamed at Pilate, they were shouting hatred and murder. They were demanding punishment, revenge and a spectacular killing. Their voices became so demanding that Pilate felt he had to give in. I am not afraid to say that he regretted his choice. Later on he decided to have a sign made and put on the cross. The sign read: Jesus, king of the Jews. The mob urged him to change that statement, to them it was blasphemy. Surely Jesus was not the king of the Jews; He only claimed to be so. Pilate was stubborn and held on to the truth he learned when Jesus stood before him and talked about His Kingdom. He found this man intriguing and wanted to learn more from Him. Of course the crowd saw Pilate's hesitation and subtle interest in Jesus and they warned him, saying,

Anyone who claims to be a king is a rebel against the Emperor (John 19:12).

In other words: 'Look governor, you have a rebel on your hands, don't you get it?' But Pilate ignored their cries and looked one more time at Jesus. This man was the king of the Jews, yet they wanted to kill Him. What a crazy world. Where had it gone wrong? Meanwhile the crowd kept shouting at Pilate, their voices so loud, so angry, so unreasonable… What was he supposed to do? Pilate finally gave in to pressure and handed Jesus over. In a last desperate try to speak up for Jesus he did not deny His kingship when he said to the people (John 19:14b):

Here is your king.

Looking back at Pilate and Peter (what a pair by the way) I wonder how it was possible for both of them to deny Jesus in the last moment. Pilate tried, but he couldn't stand up for the truth. Peter didn't even try. I believe they were both distracted by everything going on around them. The air was filled with accusations. Earlier Pilate had asked the crowd (John 18:29)

What do you accuse this man of?

From the beginning of Jesus's ministry on earth the religious establishment had been looking for ways to accuse Him falsely. Their charges confused Pilate. Surely they were not true, surely this man before him was not guilty of anything they said. Peter had to deal with his share of accusations too. They blamed him for being with Jesus, for being a disciple and for being in the garden at the arrest of Jesus. Although all these statements were true, they sounded like verdicts to Peter. The way they were hurled at him was frightening and he denied what was being said. Both Pilate and Peter knew the truth, but the voices surrounding them brought confusion. They could not think straight anymore. The charges became louder than the truth and they gave in.

Personally, I believe Pilate knew the truth but there were clearly too many distracting voices that deceived him and therefore he gave in. Revelation 12:9 tells us that the ancient serpent, named the devil or Satan, has deceived the whole world. Wow, that includes you, me and everyone, not just Pilate. Satan deceives people by telling lies and he accuses people of things they have not done. No wonder Jesus calls him a liar, even the father of all lies (John 8:44). In Revelation 12:10 he is called the accuser. Yes, the devil has various names. He is known as a liar, an accuser and a deceiver. All names that reflect his character.

Now, the Bible tells us that Jesus has the Name above all names (Phil. 2:9). So whoever or whatever else has a name in heaven or on earth, none equals the name of Jesus. Jesus has many names and each one of them symbolizes part of His character. Most people are familiar with the 'Good Shepherd', the 'Light of the World', the 'Bread of Life' and the 'Lamb' for example. Each name tells a story which comforts us in the seasons of our lives. Each name is a metaphor. The Son of God is compared with bread, with water and with life. Jesus liked to talk in parables and metaphors. However, He spoke very plainly when He said

I am the way, the truth, and the life

as recorded in John 14:6. I am the truth! Well, that teaches us truth is not a statement or a written code, a set of rules or even a conscience, it is a person. Jesus Christ is the truth the whole world is looking for. Jesus is God and He never changes, which makes Truth with a capital T an absolute. It is the foundation of everything we believe in and it is the framework that holds our worldview. The world believes that truth is based on feelings: if it feels good, it is good. This point of view makes truth very variable. The sad fact is that many Christians have embraced this thought as well. They no longer believe in absolute truth. How can that be? Jesus is truth. He breathes it, He speaks it, He acts it. If we want to know the truth, we must get to know Him! We must learn from Him, listen to Him, talk with Him, obey Him and in doing so we will get to know the truth better and closer and more intimate and more real.

Jesus told Pilate in John 18:37

I was born and came into the world for this one purpose, to speak about the truth.

Being the truth, He could do nothing else than speak in all honesty. He spoke according to His very nature. Jesus came to our world with this one purpose in mind: to speak about the truth. Why? Because He knew the people needed it then and He knows how much we still need it now! He knew that people would be lost without proper direction and He knows we are still getting lost when we leave the Way, the Truth and the Life.

Centuries had passed since the events in the Garden of Eden and the world had become a messy place. It was time for truth to invade the world and yet, many did not recognize Him when He came. Lies and deception covered the minds of the people. The Son of the living God came to earth to speak about the truth. Yet, the people accused Him of being a liar, a fraud, even an accomplice of Beelzebul. They exchanged truth for a lie. Crazy, if we think about it now. But quite honestly, we can still see this happening today.

We live in a messy world as well. Sadly enough many people have wandered away from God's moral standards and have exchanged the truth for a lie. It is even more disturbing that we also see this among people who proclaim to be Christians. They are deceived of course. The Apostle Peter saw it coming and wrote,

Many will follow their immoral ways; and because of what they do, others will speak evil of the Way of truth (2 Peter 2:2).

We see this happening on a worldwide scale: scandals within the church. Scandals concerning money laundering, immoral behavior, manipulation etc. etc. The church, and thus God, is getting a bad name because of such practices. The Bible says 'others will speak evil of the Way of truth', which is Jesus of course. This has to stop! If as a church we have wandered away from the truth, how can we expect 'others' to find the very One they need most?

Today, people might recognize Jesus as a good teacher, a nice man, a prophet even… but when Christians claim that He is the absolute Truth, with a capital T, many do not want to accept this. Maybe because embracing truth would mean embracing Jesus and His teachings. And that means we can no longer bow down to deception.

Now, the world has a clever way of feeding the masses with deception. For example, when we hear certain statements often and long enough, we begin to accept them as truth without researching for ourselves. This is how modern media often manipulates the minds of people. They do it with commercials, with political slogans and with so-called background news. Repetition is the key to pollute the minds of the public. Creating hypes is another effective tool to mess with our thinking. We have to be so careful not to repeat what we hear through the grapevine, on the news, or in church for that matter, without checking the validity of the message. We can do so by checking it with biblical truth. We must study truth in order to intercept a lie.

Contrary to Jesus's nature we have seen what the nature of the devil is. Jesus says about him in John 8:44

When he tells a lie, he is only doing what is natural to him, because he is a liar and the father of all lies.

When the devil tried to tempt Jesus (Matthew 4) he started off by saying: 'if you are God's Son', in other words 'if that is true'. Whenever Jesus opened His mouth He always kept putting emphasis on His words by adding 'I am telling you the truth'. I am sure that if you listened to Him long enough you got a clue of what the truth was all about.

So far we have seen that according to the Bible, Jesus

- is the Truth with a capital T
- came to speak about truth and
- came to make the Law and teachings come true.

Somehow, that mission was the reason why certain people wanted to kill Him. Maybe the people of that time did not want to hear what He had to say. Maybe they had made up their own so-called 'truth' or maybe they simply didn't want the truth to be a person. Whatever the reason, their attitude even boggles Jesus. Just check out their arguments all through the 8th chapter in the book of John. In verse 45 Jesus fires away at them,

But I tell the truth, and that is <u>why</u> you do not believe me.

He raises the following question in verse 47

If I tell the truth, then <u>why</u> do you not believe me?

Good question. Wouldn't you think they were able to recognize truth when spoken? Were they somehow blinded or deceived? Maybe they had expected truth to come in a scroll or a prayer cloth or even written on the wall by God's hand. This might be a good moment to ask ourselves what we would answer if Jesus asked us that 'why' question. Why do you not believe Me? You see, Jesus tells us not to worry, not to fear and not to fret. Why don't we believe Him when He says so? Jesus tells us to forgive others as often as we need to. Why then, do we not believe Him? Why then, do we often not obey

Jesus's teaching? One of Jesus's most profound statements can be found in John 13:34,

And now I give you a new commandment: love one another. As I have loved you, so you must love one another.

That is a commandment, a new one for that matter. So many Christians are allergic to the word 'commandment'. They think it is an Old Testament word that no longer has any value for the modern day believer. How is it possible that Christians want to delete that word when Jesus uses it, all the time? He uses it even, or should I say specifically, in combination with love.

Love is the truth Jesus spoke about and love is the fulfillment or implementation of the Law (Romans 13:10 NIV). Every time we act in love, we live according to God's law. We actually live truth and we deny falsehood. One of the names of God is 'Love' (1 John 4:8). God equals love in the same way as Jesus equals truth. If He would stand before us today and spoke about the truth, about loving one another, would we believe Him? If He would stand before us today and spoke about not harming one another, would we believe Him? Would we obey Him?

We would probably discover that His truth is miles away from our reality. We have often grown so accustomed to reading gossip, to watching shows where people get accused and blamed for all kinds of things. We don't even think twice when we hear of frivolous lawsuits which are not about the truth, but all about the money and the media attention. We are being fed on a daily basis with all kinds of lies and gossip. Gossip that hurts the people involved, news that defiles people's names, political lies and stories that blame fellow humans for things they have never done. We take it in, we consume it and it fills us up. Of Jesus it was said that He was full of truth. How about us? What are we full of?

Truth will come out of us when it is stored up in our hearts. If we are full of truth, we can stand up for it. We must, however, make a conscious decision to stop listening to lies, accusations and gossip and spend time filling up with the Word. This means turning off the television when needed, unsubscribe certain magazines or no longer hang out with people who engage in such practices. We can make the decision today to change our diet and feast on truth!

Meditate on the following:

❖ *What are my favorite television shows, magazines and books? What attracts me in it?*

❖ *How much time do I spend filling my mind and heart with truth (Bible reading, prayer etc.)?How does that compare with the time I spend being entertained?*

❖ *Am I quick to accuse someone?(let's call it 'judging')*

Journal your thoughts:

6

Treasure of good things

He gives you food and fills your hearts with happiness

Acts 14:17b

Of Jesus it was said that He was full of grace and truth. What about us? What has taken up the space in our hearts? We can be full of joy, doubt, fear, hatred, love or compassion. Whatever is growing in our hearts, will eventually become the fruit of our lips.

Maybe we are not always aware of this, but when we speak, we speak of things that we have taken in and stored up. We can have good or bad things in our hearts. Jesus said it like this:

A good person brings good out of the treasure of good things in his heart; a bad person brings bad out of his treasure of bad things. For the mouth speaks what the heart is full of (Luke 6:45).

With the mouth we give voice to what is in the heart. No wonder God urges us not to accuse anyone falsely or should we say: no wonder the Spirit urges us to speak the truth at all times. The Bible teaches extensively about the things we should or shouldn't say. Proverbs 18:21 for example,

The tongue has the power of life and death.

It is therefore not just words leaving my mouth when I speak, it is power. Our words have the power to build up or to break down. In the third chapter of James we can read how the tongue is compared to the rudder of a big ship, it goes wherever the captain commands it to go. So, the question is, where are our words taking us? Are they taking us on a path of destruction and never ending drama or are they taking us to a higher level of living? It all depends on what we have stored up in our hearts.

Quite simply, if we want to speak the truth whenever we talk, we have to feed ourselves on biblical truth and store up such treasures within. We must take an honest inventory. As long as we are feeding ourselves with false accusations, either by watching it, listening to it, reading about it or even speaking it, we cannot expect that healthy, truthful words will come over our lips when we speak. Isaiah 14:29 gives us a piece of typical eastern wisdom on this;

A snake's egg hatches a flying dragon.

Be careful what you play with! Bad gives birth to worse. If we want to store up truth, we have to be around truth. We have to fill ourselves up with it.

Jesus taught some interesting lessons about this subject. He said:

The eye is the lamp of the body. If your eyes are good, your whole body will be full of light (Matthew 6:22).

He is talking about our fixation here. He is talking about the things that attract our attention. Are our eyes glued to the television screen, questionable websites, violent movies, other people's possessions or talents? Are the images and words we pick up with our eyes good or bad, positive or negative? What do we read? Do we delight in reading gossip? Do we silently enjoy reading about the misery in the lives of celebrities? Do we fill our minds with lies, false accusations or perversity? Do we toss and turn and lay awake at night as a result of the 'dark' episode we were watching before turning the lights off? Jesus describes our eyes as the entrance for either defiling or enlightening our bodies. In other words: watch what you watch! Watch what you read! We should guard our natural vision in order to build up our spiritual vision. Fixing our ears and eyes on the truth will fill us with the truth. As Jesus told Pilate,

Whoever belongs to the truth listens to me (John 18:37).

Truth is personified in the Son Of God who came to us in the form of a person; someone who lived and moved among the people of the earth. Truth came in the form of a person who befriended the outlaws of society, the sick, the desperate, the lonely and the lost. He befriended them so they would learn the truth from Him. By being among the common people Jesus had a chance to show what truth was all about. He said things they had never heard before and He did things they had never seen before. Up until His coming into their world, religious people had been living by the Law. If any dispute arose or difficult questions were being asked, they consulted the teachers of the Law who knew all the answers. Jesus however turned their world upside down when He told them the following:

If you do obey my teaching, you are really my disciples; you will know the truth, and the truth will set you free (John 8:31-32).

What in the world was He talking about? Did He claim to have a different teaching then the one that was handed down by their forefathers? Was He contradicting the Law of Moses and the teaching of the Prophets? No, of course not. Jesus explained that the Law that was handed down kept them in bondage. He gave them a sneak preview at the redemptive work on the cross. Only the Son can set people free; not the Law.

It is one of the most important truths Jesus came to talk about. In Matthew 5:17 He made that very clear when He said,

Do not think that I have come to do away with the Law of Moses and the teachings of the prophets. I have not come to do away with them, but to make their teachings come true!

He came for that purpose, to make the teachings come true. Therefore truth is not a written statement, it is a person; it lives, it moves, it exists. Now, if Jesus claimed to be the truth we should be able to learn a thing or two from Him because many of His words and actions have been written down. Let us take a closer look at the life and the words of the only person who never fell for deception.

Most people are familiar with the birth of Jesus as depicted in the gospel of Luke. Personally I like the version of the disciple John much better. Nothing wrong with the virgin Mary, the angels and shepherds of course, but John has a way of telling the same story from a totally different perspective, a spiritual perspective. He starts off with a very powerful statement in verse 1,

Before the world was created, the Word already existed; He was with God, and He was the same as God.

In verse 14 he tells us about the birth of Jesus,

The Word became a human being, and, full of grace and truth, lived among us.

In so little words John explains the Bible. Jesus existed even before the world was made; therefore His human birth was not the beginning of His existence. He was the same as God, but His earthly birth gave Him a different glory. The glory He received as the Father's only son. Last but not least, Jesus is also called the Word. Right at the beginning of his book the apostle John tells us that Jesus was full of grace and truth and in verse 17 he adds that grace and truth came through Jesus. John recognized the truth in Jesus. His writings are proof that Jesus came indeed to talk about the truth. At least twenty five times John describes a situation where Jesus says: *I am telling you the truth.* The KJV says 'verily, verily, I say unto thee'. I looked up 'verily' in Webster's dictionary since it is a word we hardly use anymore; it simply means 'in very truth'. Somehow Jesus always impressed upon the people that what He was saying was the truth. He did so one more time while standing before Pilate (John 18:37),

I was born and came into the world for this one purpose, to speak about the truth.

Jesus exists eternally. He was, is and is to come. He was there before the foundation of the earth was established. Yet, He came to earth as a human being, a baby born of a young virgin mother. He came personally to the earth, sent by God the Father with a purpose: to speak about the truth. People in the Middle East had Him right in their midst and He spoke very clearly with them about the issues of daily life.

For us, people of the 21st century, it is all different. Jesus is no longer with us in person. He went back to the Father and is seated at the right hand of God. Therefore truth is no longer with us in person. Now, this is not a permission to make up our own truth. When Jesus left, He gave His followers a very clear mandate,

I am telling you the truth: those who believe in me will do what I do—yes, they will do even greater things, because I am going to the Father (John 14:12).

When Jesus walked the earth, He filled every room and every space with His presence. He spoke about the truth constantly. We walk the earth too; some of us never get any further than the outskirts of town, while others fly from continent to continent. The question remains, what do we speak about? What kind of impression do we leave behind? Are we messengers of truth?

Meditate on the following:

❖ *What are my favorite topics of conversation?*

❖ *How do I fill up my heart with good things?*

❖ *What action can I take to watch what I watch?*

Journal your thoughts:

7

Spirit of truth

"I am telling you the truth," replied Jesus, "that no one can enter the Kingdom of God without being born of water and the Spirit."

John 3:5

When reading through the previous chapters we might wonder if it is possible to be full of truth, as Jesus was. After all, we may no longer be of this world, but we are still in it and we are being polluted by it, sometimes even without realizing. Where will our help come from?

Pilate proclaimed three times that he could find no fault in Jesus. Peter proclaimed three times that he did not know Jesus. Both men knew the truth, but gave in to people's pressure and fear which kept them from speaking truth. Leading up to His trial before Pilate and the denial of Peter, Jesus proclaimed three times that a Helper was on the way: the Spirit of truth. Let us take a closer look at these three powerful and very important declarations as recorded in chapters 14, 15 and 16 of the book of John.

John 14:16-17

The first time Jesus mentions the coming of the Spirit of truth is right after He predicts Peter's denial. In John 14:16-17 we can read the following announcement:

I will ask the Father, and he will give you another Helper, who will stay with you forever. He is the Spirit, who reveals the truth about God. The world cannot receive him, because it cannot see him or know him. But you know him, because he remains with you and is in you.

Now that is a miniature Good News message in itself. First of all it shows the close connection between Jesus and His Father. They obviously communicate and there is room for questions; Jesus says He will *ask* the Father. At the same time there is also confidence in God answering His request: 'He *will* give another Helper'. That is awesome news. The Spirit who reveals the truth about God will be given to us and will stay with us forever. The NIV translation calls Him the Spirit of truth. There is just one restriction…. The world cannot receive Him. What exactly does this mean? If there is one thing the world needs, it is the Spirit of truth. It would solve many if not all problems and end all disputes. Yet Jesus clearly says the world cannot receive Him because they cannot see or know Him.

I believe He says this because the receiving of the Holy Spirit in one's life is not a mass happening on a worldwide scale, it is no corporate business. The receiving of the Holy Spirit is a personal matter between a man or a woman and God. On an individual basis any person, no matter what color, race, background or age, who puts his or her faith in Jesus Christ becomes a child of God and will receive the Holy Spirit as a mark of ownership. The apostle Paul describes this miracle in Ephesians 1:13 as follows:

And you also became God's people when you heard the true message, the Good News that brought you salvation. You believed in Christ, and God put his stamp of ownership on you by giving you the Holy Spirit he had promised.

People, who do not believe in Jesus Christ do not have the Holy Spirit and quite frankly, they do not understand spiritual things because God has not enlightened them. I remember this clearly in my own life. Although I grew up in a Christian family and went to church and Sunday school as a child, I was not enlightened. I was a name Christian by birth, simply because my parents and grandparents were Christians. Later on in life I had to make my own choice to believe in Jesus Christ and that took me a long time, because I was stubborn and thought I could live any way I wanted. But God's love caught up with me and I fell on my knees and admitted that I wanted to step down from the throne of my life. I admitted that I needed Him to sit on that throne and take over because I was making a mess of things and quite frankly on my way to nowhere.

What a wonderful moment in my life, not a single day has been the same since. My eyes were opened instantly for His truth and His Word. Everything that I had regarded as nonsense up to that point became clear. I had received the Spirit of truth. One day while reading my Bible I came across 1 Corinthians 2:14 and saw truth more clearly than ever before:

Whoever does not have the Spirit cannot receive the gifts that come from God's Spirit. Such a person really does not understand them, and they seem to be nonsense, because their value can be judged only on a spiritual basis.

Wow, this is so true and so vital. If we do not understand this, we will judge and blame people for being blind to God's truth while the fact of the matter is that they cannot see the things of God. In the words of Jesus in John 14:16-17: the world cannot receive the Spirit of God, the Spirit of truth, only people who put their faith and trust in God. Some people make the decision to do so when they are young, others (like me) postpone this surrender to God for years! How and when it happens is up to God and up to the free will decision of every person. The most important thing is *that* it happens. Intercessory prayer for our loved ones to make this decision is therefore very valuable.

Now Jesus furthermore said that we will know the Spirit because He remains with us and is in us. Getting to know someone is a result of spending time together, talking, listening and asking questions. I like to call that: to hang out with someone. So, how do we hang out with God's Spirit of truth? How do we get to know Him better? Well, first of all we need to communicate. For many Christians the Holy Spirit is rather vague. Many would describe Him as a wind, fire, force or dove. But these are only symbols, it is not who He is! The Holy Spirit is God, just as Jesus is God. Jesus is not a piece of bread, a vine or a rock… these are symbols to describe who He is, to describe His character. In the same way, symbols are being used to describe the character of the Holy Spirit, who is a person. An invisible person that is. We can listen to Him, we can grieve Him, we can invite Him and yes, we can talk with Him on a daily basis. We can have fellowship with Him because He lives in us and remains in us. So, when Jesus said that we are able to know the Spirit, He was talking about establishing a relationship. It is no more than common sense that we have to get to know the One that has taken up residence in our bodies.

I would like to urge you to make communication with the Holy Spirit part of your daily life. Call Him by name and say 'Holy Spirit, Spirit of truth, you are my Helper and I need help, all the time. Today, I need help with my work, my mother in law, my dietary discipline…' whatever the case. Ask Him for revelation on matters you have been thinking about. Ask Him for inspiration when you want to be creative. Ask Him to reveal truth in pressing matters. Ask Him to show you the heart of God. He is the Spirit who reveals the truth about God. We can ask Him anything!

It took me many years, lots of Bible reading and several good books about fellowship with the Holy Spirit, before I was able to engage with Him on a daily basis. My religious upbringing and background did not teach me anything about a relationship with the Holy Spirit. Yet, each Sunday in church we received the blessing as written in 2 Corinthians 13:13,

The grace of the Lord Jesus Christ, the love of God, and the fellowship of the Holy Spirit be with you all.

The fellowship of the Holy Spirit… I never gave it a second thought and millions of churchgoers with me. Fellowship means communion, companionship, camaraderie, friendship, partnership, mutuality. We are supposed to build a relationship with Him, just as people befriended Jesus when He walked around the Sea of Galilee and towards Jerusalem. The Holy Spirit wants to be our friend and teach us everything about truth.

Personally I believe it should not take us many years and lots of study to enjoy this fellowship, it should come naturally when we begin to communicate with Him. We have made things too complicated. We can embrace His invitation as a child. If you have never had a conversation with the Holy Spirit, begin by asking Him to reveal truth about a matter that has been on your heart or mind for a long time.

Jesus went on with His speech and said:

The Helper, the Holy Spirit, whom the Father will send in my name, will teach you everything and make you remember all that I have told you (John 14:26)

He is willing to teach us everything! Do we truly realize what a great and wonderful gift has been given to us? We have truth living in us as a teacher. He will never ever say anything that does not come from God. He will give us revelation, inspiration and clarification about all issues of life and faith.

The Holy Spirit will make us remember all that Jesus has taught. Have you ever had that happen? You are in a conversation with someone and suddenly words come out that are so right on! Words that are exactly to the point and accurate and you wonder... where did that come from? Where did I get that kind of wisdom? Well, that is the Holy Spirit at work. He brings to remembrance the teachings of Jesus and He gives us the right words to speak at the right time. It is truly a delight when that happens and I believe God wants it to happen all the time! Personally, I experience this frequently during corporate prayer times when we pray in a group for a certain issue or topic. Scriptures come to my mind as a flow of words to pray and proclaim. I do not need to struggle to pray good prayers or to say the right words; the Holy Spirit brings God's promises and principles to my mind. This is His good pleasure and I love it when that happens. He truly is our Helper.

John 15:26

The second time Jesus announces the coming of the Spirit of truth can be found in John 15:26. It is almost as if He wants to put emphasis on the fact that His followers will not be left behind all alone:

The Helper will come—the Spirit, who reveals the truth about God and who comes from the Father. I will send him to you from the Father, and he will speak about me.

Again, it is clear that this Spirit of truth comes from the Father, or should I say 'comes from Heaven'. He does not come unannounced, uninvited or on His own accord, but only because Jesus will send Him. This gift from Heaven is the power of God to transform our lives. He transforms us from slaves (sin, shame, guilt and fear) into sons and daughters of God. He makes us family, as written in Galatians 4:6-7,

To show that you are his children, God sent the Spirit of his Son into our hearts, the Spirit who cries out, "Father, my Father." So then, you are no longer a slave but a child. And since you are his child, God will give you all that he has for his children.

So, the Spirit is a God sent. He is His gift to us just as Jesus is His gift to mankind. We certainly do not deserve such divine, royal gifts, but God is good and gracious and desires to give us the best, as any loving parent would do for his or her child.

Now, the question is 'in what manner do we receive this gift?' Are we appreciative for the fact that the Holy Spirit wants to make our bodies His home or do we take His presence for granted? I often ask people whether the Holy Spirit is living in them, whether they have fellowship with Him on a daily basis and whether they learn from Him. It never stops to amaze me how often I get the answer that people are not really sure, that they are not fully aware that it is the Spirit who enables us to call God our Father. It never stops to amaze me that many Christians hardly ever communicate with the Spirit who lives in them, the Spirit that was given as a helper, a counselor, a teacher and a comforter. It seems we receive God's gift the way we sometimes receive earthly gifts. We are happy and excited for a moment, but when the novelty wears off we forget and the gift ends up in the corner. Doesn't it make sense to give Him a warm welcome, like we would do when it was Jesus Himself? He then will begin to speak to us. He will speak about Jesus. How awesome is that? He will speak truth deep into our hearts; we will be filled up to overflowing with truth.

It is my personal experience and conviction that the Holy Spirit often speaks quietly. He doesn't scream. Jesus says that He will reveal the truth about God. To reveal, to give revelation. We don't want to miss this if we want to learn more about God's truthful character which He desires to see alive in us. This is why we need to shut down other voices that do *not* speak the truth so as to give Him more and more room to converse with us. It might come down to turning off the radio, television, internet, phones and other gadgets that are not proclaiming truth. It might come down to temporarily walking away from friends, family or others that are *not* speaking the truth. We should not argue, fight or judge them. Just be kind, but at the same time protect our eye and ear gates from what is coming in. When we are no longer ruled by what others (and that may be the media or our own family members) are saying but only by what the Spirit is saying, we will speak truth! The apostle Paul came to that point. He describes it in Romans 9:1,

I am speaking the truth; I belong to Christ and I do not lie. My conscience, ruled by the Holy Spirit, also assures me that I am not lying...

Oh yes, it is possible for you to come to that point as well. Our conscience should be ruled by the Spirit of truth, no longer by circumstances, experiences, opinions or by other voices as we have seen in Pilate's and Peter's case. To be ruled by the Holy Spirit means that we submit to His leading, to His unctions and promptings. It means we follow His directions and often they are subtle!

John 16:13

The third time Jesus announces the coming of the Spirit of truth is in John 16:13-14. Aside from emphasizing the coming of the Spirit of truth, He adds here that the Spirit will tell us of things to come and that He will give glory to Jesus.

When, however, the Spirit comes, who reveals the truth about God, he will lead you into all the truth. He will not speak on his own authority, but he will speak of what he hears and will tell you of things to come. He will give me glory, because he will take what I say and tell it to you.

The Spirit who reveals the truth about God or, as some translations say, the Spirit of truth will lead us into all truth. How long will it take before we are lead into all truth? I don't know. It might be a lifelong process, but if Jesus promises it, I believe it will come to pass. To be lead into all truth means that bit by bit, piece by piece we will gain understanding and insight about the very things of God. We will learn about His character, His desires and His love. It means that we will receive revelation about Jesus, His Son. It surely means we will be surprised and encouraged each time He reveals truth to us.

The Holy Spirit, or Spirit of truth, will not speak on His own authority; He will only speak of what He hears. Now, that is exactly how Jesus operated when He was on earth. In John 8:28 Jesus says,

When you lift up the Son of Man, you will know that 'I am who I am'; then you will know that I do nothing on my own authority, but I say only what the Father has instructed me to say.

This is so wonderful. Jesus does not speak on His own authority and the same is true for the Holy Spirit. They will only speak of what they hear the Father say. They are in communion with each other and they are in agreement with each other. There is not a single reason to fear the Holy Spirit. I meet many Christians who are afraid of God's Spirit. They have been taught to be careful and not to put too much emphasis on Him, as other believers do. They even believe the manifestations of the Spirit's work on earth are from the evil one. There is NO scriptural basis for such warnings and I would like to urge all believers to research the Scriptures on the person and works of the Holy Spirit. He is God's gift to mankind. Please, do not refuse Him.

It is interesting to read what Jesus furthermore had to say,

And he who sent me is with me; he has not left me alone, because I always do what pleases him (John 8:29).

Jesus always does what pleases God. Earlier in this book we saw that the same applies to believers; we should try to find out what pleases the Lord. Now, the Holy Spirit is no exception to this. He never speaks on His own authority. So, we can be assured that the Spirit of truth will speak to us on all occasions with a message directly from God, with a message that has the approval of God. He will even tell us of things to come! That does not make the Holy Spirit a fortune teller, but it surely makes Him a messenger from Heaven. It means He will be able to warn us from upcoming danger. He will be able to guide us in the way we should go. He will be able to correct us when leaving the right path etc. etc.

Another wonderful thing the Holy Spirit will do is bring glory to Jesus because He will take what Jesus says and tell it to us. The Spirit of truth that lives in us takes whatever Jesus says or said and communicates it to us. All too often we expect God to speak from Heaven, we hope for a voice that will clearly tell us yes or no. We wait for a sign, a word or even a whisper from above. My husband once said that every now and then he would like to see one of those small planes flying over pulling a banner with God's answer. He said this, because we sometimes struggle hearing God's voice. We are impatient and we want Him to use the methods we are familiar with: clear answers, written notes or an audible voice. I am not saying that God will never work that way, but He has given us the Helper, the Spirit who will interconnect us with God. He is a transmitter. He will tell us of things to come. He will tell us what He hears from Jesus and in doing so He will bring glory to Jesus. We cannot ignore the role of the Spirit of truth in us, He is our essential companion.

If we want to learn truth we must learn to listen to the Holy Spirit and not to the many voices in the world.... simply because the world does not know Him.

Meditate on the following:

- *How can I activate communication with the Holy Spirit?*

- *Is there an area in my life where I need Truth with a capital T to be revealed?*

- *Which voices are of influence in my life on a daily basis?*

Journal your thoughts:

8

Obedience redefined

You were doing so well! Who made you stop obeying the truth?

Galatians 5:7

It all sounds wonderful, don't you think? When we give our hearts to Jesus, He will give us the Holy Spirit, the Spirit of truth, and we can't go wrong… ever. If it is that easy why are we often struggling to understand truth, why do we even get deceived from time to time? Why is it not always the truth that I speak?

Let us go back to the words of Jesus while standing before Pilate. He said (John 18:38),

Whoever belongs to the truth listens to Me.

We already established the fact that Jesus *is* truth. So, He is basically saying to Pilate that whoever belongs to Him should listen to Him! My first reaction to these words was: duh! Whoever belongs to Jesus surely listens to Jesus. To whom else would we listen? But then it dawned on me… Jesus does not automatically assume that everyone who belongs to Him is also listening to what He is saying. We might *know* what He is saying, we might *hear* what He is saying, we might *read* what He is saying. We might even *talk* about it. But the important question is: are we doing what He says? In other words: are we being obedient? Jesus said a little earlier (John 14:15):

If you love me, you will obey my commandments.

We don't like to hear that, but that is really what our Lord meant. Listening to Jesus, listening to truth, means doing what He says, no exceptions. He continues His speech with the following words,

Whoever has my commands and obeys them, he is the one who loves me (John 14:21, NIV).

I always love it when the Bible uses the word 'whoever'. It doesn't exclude anyone. Whatever promise or principle follows that word is applicable to every person no matter what age, race, gender, background or upbringing. Whoever obeys Jesus is the one who loves Him. Whoever belongs to the truth listens to Jesus and no longer to his or her own desires. To belong to the truth really means to belong to God. So, how can a person know for sure that he or she belongs to God? We can know it by the Spirit who lives in us. This is being described in 1 John 3:24 [emphasis mine],

Whoever [there is that word again] *obeys God's commands lives in union with God and God lives in union with him. And <u>because of the Spirit</u> that God has given us <u>we know</u> that God lives in union with us.*

It doesn't really matter how we came to a living faith in God, as long as we *know* that we have received the Holy Spirit. When people come to a radical decision for Christ in their life, it is often easy to point out the date and time when that happened. When asked to give their testimony they will have a very specific story of repentance, forgiveness and rebirth. However, when people have been in church for most of their lives, it is often more difficult to point out the moment in time when their faith became personal, when it no longer was the faith of their parents or grandparents that kept them going. I grew up in a Christian family and went to church and Sunday school when I was young. However, when I was sixteen years of age, I decided to go my own way. I still believed in God, I still read the Bible regularly, but I did not live a life pleasing to God. I had never confessed my sin, never understood the need for a Savior and did not come to a turning point in my life until I was almost forty years old. And even then it was not a matter of a spectacular conversion.

Looking back I can see that God's Spirit was working on my heart for months, before I finally allowed Him to come in, before I finally came to the point where I was willing to surrender and let go of the reigns of my life. A few weeks later I was present at an evangelistic campaign and I stepped forward in the crowd to (literally) give my life to Jesus, although that had probably already happened several months before. It was a done deal in the spiritual realm, but I added a step of practical faith to His love and grace offer by moving out of my seat, stepping forward, raising my hand and confessing with my mouth what I already believed in my heart. I had received the Holy Spirit as His stamp of ownership and from that moment on I wanted to be ruled by His Spirit, no longer by my own desires, emotions and reasoning.

Now, this is a point that some believers never really get to; giving the reigns over to the Holy Spirit, the Spirit of truth who lives in us. So often, we want Jesus as our savior, as our comforter and helper but not as our Lord. I believe this is what Jesus talks about when He says: 'whoever belongs to the truth listens to Me'. It is one thing to have Him in our hearts; it is another thing to do as He tells us to!

Having the Spirit of truth take up residence in our lives, does not automatically mean we will be clean of all deception. It does not automatically mean we will know all truth. The key is that we have to obey! What good is it to belong to Jesus and not do as He says? That would be like saying; 'we love you Jesus, but we do not want to follow your commands...' This is exactly what is happening all over the world and it results in a watered-down Christianity. My husband and I travel a lot and it doesn't matter which country we visit, we always meet people who, for example, belong to the school of thought that we no longer need to confess our sins. When Jesus died on the cross He took the sins of the whole world upon His shoulders. Past, present and future sins. If we accept His grace there is no longer a need to be worried about sin. Now, I do underline the thought that as believers we should indeed not be sin-conscious. Sin should no longer be on our mind because by the grace of God we have received the righteousness of God. So we should be righteousness-conscious, which means knowing for sure that nothing can separate us from the love of Christ. But the Bible clearly states that we should not act as if sin no longer exists. In 1 John 1:8 we can find a clear warning against this way of thinking,

If we say that we have no sin, we deceive ourselves, and there is no truth in us.

There you have it, the theme of this book! Deception will keep us from living in truth. John is talking to believers here, people who already have been forgiven, people who already have received the Holy Spirit, the Spirit of truth. Yet, it is possible to become deceived simply by not being serious about sin. I hope we will take His words seriously. The next two verses on this topic are also very powerful,

But if we confess our sins to God, he will keep his promise and do what is right: he will forgive us our sins and purify us from all our wrongdoing. If we say that we have not sinned, we make a liar out of God, and his word is not in us.

If we say we have not sinned, we make a liar out of God. We would be doing the work of Satan. Remember the scene in the Garden of Eden? We must be very careful not to let deception enter our minds. We must stick to the truth and nothing but the truth. The apostle Paul is concerned about believers swaying back and forth with every new wind of teaching. He writes in 2 Corinthians 11:3 (NIV),

But I am afraid that just as Eve was deceived by the serpent's cunning, your minds may somehow be led astray from your sincere and pure devotion to Christ.

Again we see deception going back all the way to the Garden of Eden where it all started. The Bible tells us that in the last days the word, the truth will be twisted and many people will be deceived. Please, make sure you are not one of them. You must read the Word for yourself and talk with the Spirit of truth who has taken up residence in your heart. He will guide you into all truth if you decide to listen.

By the way, listening in Biblical terms is so much more than just hearing a word, it is listening and doing! James 1:22 says,

Do not deceive yourselves by just listening to his word; instead put it into practice.

In this book we have seen that it is the work of the enemy to deceive people. Here we see that it is also possible to deceive ourselves. Now that is something else. Do not deceive yourselves… it is a stern warning from the apostle James to believers scattered over the whole world. This letter was written in the first century after Christ and somehow there were believers who had the habit of listening to the word but not acting upon it. James calls it deception. When we think that by listening to a sermon or teaching or by reading from the Bible we have done our 'duty, we are deceived. We must put into practice what we have learned. Let's read verse 25,

But whoever looks closely into the perfect law that sets people free, who keeps on paying attention to it and does not simply listen and then forget it, but puts it into practice-that person will be blessed by God in what he does.

James talks about the perfect law that sets people free. This is not the 9th Commandment! We have seen in this book that obeying or keeping the Law is not the same as fulfilling it. Not giving false testimony is one thing, speaking truth is another thing. That is the law that sets people free, the law of love. There is more than simply listening to what Jesus says; we must put it into practice. I truly believe this is what Jesus was getting to when He stood before Pilate. Let's face it, Pilate was listening to Jesus, he wanted Him to speak up. He wanted to hear words of truth from His lips. He was willing to listen, but he was not willing to do what Jesus said. He was not willing to follow and obey Him.

If we belong to Christ, we must do as He says. This is, or should be, the heart of modern Christianity. Jesus is the Truth, with a capital T. If we belong to the truth, we must do as He says which is called 'obedience'. We don't like that word, basically as much as we don't like the word 'commandment'. I am not afraid to say that if obedience disappears out of our society, truth will disappear. Reading through biblical history this has happened again and again. In the seventh chapter of the book of the prophet Jeremiah for example, we can read about the disobedience of the people. Verse 28 says,

This is the nation that has not obeyed the Lord its God or responded to correction. Truth has perished; it has vanished from their lips.

Truth had perished because no one was willing to respond to correction. What a tragedy! Do you see history repeating itself? If we are not careful, truth will vanish from our lips as well. Let's wake up and stand up for truth. I hope my writings about Jesus have challenged you. I hope you can and will see that obedience to His commands is not something negative or scary or outdated or legalistic… it is TRUTH.

I almost feel like I am pleading, together with the early apostles, for believers not to sway back and forth with every wave of popular teaching, but to hold on to the truth. In 1 John 4:6 we can read the following,

We are from God, and whoever knows God listens to us; but whoever is not from God does not listen to us. This is how we recognize the Spirit of truth and the spirit of falsehood.

Meditate on the following:

- ❖ *How can I make my faith more practical?*

- ❖ *Do I ever hear without acting?*

- ❖ *Has God been speaking to me about something that I have not followed up on yet?*

Journal your thoughts:

9

Truth on the battlefield

Love does not delight in evil but rejoices with the truth.

1 Corinthians 13:6

Looking back over the previous chapters we can conclude that truth is not a set of rules, not a philosophy, not a variable or fashionable statement. No, truth is personified in Jesus Christ who is the way, the truth and the life. And the good and awesome news is that He has asked the Father to send us the Spirit of truth.

The Spirit of truth takes up residence in every believer's life and teaches us how to live a life of truth. This life of truth is not a matter of simply pushing a button or memorizing a set of instructions. No, it is a matter of developing a relationship with and a life lead by the Spirit of truth. The apostle John wrote,

I have no greater joy than to hear that my children are walking in the truth (3 John 1:4, NIV).

To walk in truth, I love the way he phrases that. We should be walking in the truth as we are walking in the light, which really means to be aware of God's presence and principles wherever we go. Walking in truth means practicing it, living it, defending it, speaking it.

I surely believe that the fact that biblical truth is being questioned, and even ignored in our society is one of the reasons we live in such a troubled world. The fact that biblical truth is even being questioned in our churches is one of the reasons we have so many powerless gatherings and a watered-down Christianity. More and more church denominations deny absolute and biblical truth. Water baptism, miracles, healing, manifestation of the Holy Spirit, virgin birth, sin, deity of Jesus… all of this is being questioned. Now, it will do no good to blame any specific denomination, church order or theologian for that. Getting back to the theme of this book: let's not accuse anyone, but let's speak the truth! Let's make sure God's Word is firmly established in our hearts, so we can stand up for truth when needed. 1 John 4:2-3 gives us the 'how to' nuggets,

This is how you will be able to know whether it is God's Spirit: anyone who acknowledges that Jesus Christ came as a human being has the Spirit who comes from God. But anyone who denies this about Jesus does not have the Spirit from God. The spirit that he has is from the Enemy of Christ; you heard that it would come, and now it is here in the world already.

There is an enemy of Christ in our world, an enemy of truth who will try to deceive us. He will try to persuade us to give false testimony, to accuse people, to deny truth. This is the daily battle we are in. Let's therefore take up truth, it is part of the armor God has given us so we can stand and be able to resist the enemy's attacks. Ephesians 6:14 says,

So stand ready, with truth as a belt around your waist...

What does a belt do in this age? It holds up our pants. It prevents us from going around in bare buttocks. Truth will help cover our nakedness, our vulnerability. Truth will hold things together while the world is falling apart. We cannot and should not go anywhere without the belt of truth. Too often we do not fully realize we are engaged in a spiritual battle. We want to be involved in church picnics and social functions. We want to decorate our churches for Christmas and Easter. Nothing wrong with these activities which are often the highlight of our religious seasons, but they are *not* the core of the Christian faith. We want our faith to bring us peace and prosperity. We want to have a sense of belonging and safety. We often feel mistreated when attacked about our values and convictions. We complain about our Christian freedoms being taken away. How different is that kind of thinking from the attitude the first Christians had. In 2 Corinthians 6:8 the apostle Paul writes,

We are honored and disgraced; we are insulted and praised. We are treated as liars, yet we speak the truth...

They were treated as liars, yet they continued to speak the truth. They did not cry or complain, they did not back down, they did not change their theology in order to satisfy the masses. I think it is time to realize we are soldiers on a mission, not vacationers on a cruise.

Biblical truth is part of the armor God has given us and we should wear that belt. It will help us to be covered and protected from all sides. Truth Himself will surround us as we go about our business. I know from personal experience that the values, convictions and principles I live by are not the same as the ones the world is promoting. As a matter of fact, they often are opposites. It is against popular belief to stand up for biblical family values, for marriage, against abortion, against greed and idolatry. But this is what God expects from His children. If we belong to Him, we must obey Him.

We put aside all secret and shameful deeds; we do not act with deceit, nor do we falsify the word of God. In the full light of truth we live in God's sight and try to commend ourselves to everyone's good conscience (2 Corinthians 4:2).

This is pleasing to God. Let us not falsify the Word of God in order to make it more acceptable or more approachable.

When I researched the Scriptures about the Spirit of truth living in believers, I could not help but think about the tremendous positive effect we could have on a troubled world that is being deceived by the evil one. If millions and hundreds of millions of believers would allow the Spirit of truth to lead and instruct them, we would be able to push back the darkness. Truth would expose error. The devil would lose territory and more and more people would come to know the love of God. What a joyful army we could be, an army of love. 1 Corinthians 13:6 says,

Love is not happy with evil, but is happy with the truth.

Meditate on the following:

- ❖ *How do I handle my spiritual armor?*

- ❖ *How do I stand up for truth when being challenged?*

- ❖ *Write a faith statement of your fundamental biblical beliefs.*

Journal your thoughts:

10

Exhortation

The heart of your law is truth, and all your righteous judgments are eternal.

Psalm 119:160

It is my sincere hope that this book will reveal that reading the Bible or going to church, does not automatically mean we are living a life of truth. It does not automatically mean we are being obedient to Gods' heart.

As we have learned from the events in the Garden of Eden, deception (twisted truth) can creep in. Sometimes it is little stuff, for example when we do not speak the truth when asked. Let's say a friend values our opinion about a new dress or car they bought. All too often we say we love it, but we don't really mean it. Too often we find it difficult to say what is really on our hearts. Besides the fact that the Lord wants us to be honest, such 'sweet lies' are not helping the other person. Of course, it takes practice to tell the truth in love. There is a huge difference between saying 'that's an ugly dress' and 'I like it, but blue suits you better'. Sometimes the truth is painful and we have to learn to speak it in love. We can make it our habit to speak truth, but we should not forget to do it carefully and considerately when needed. The Spirit of truth will help us. If we learn to do this with little, daily things, we will practice for the really important matters of life. If we cannot stand up for small matters, how will we be able to stand up for important matters?

Apart from speaking the truth it is equally important to discern between truth and lie. So often I hear people say 'I read it in the newspaper' or 'I saw it on television' and therefore, so they conclude, the information must be true. I truly see this as one of the biggest threats to the Christian faith. Many people speak with more certainty and conviction about the daily news, than they would ever speak about God's Word. Many people find it easier to believe the weatherman than the One who holds the key to the storerooms of rain, wind and snow in His hands. Many people have an absolute trust in medical science, much more so than they trust the promises of God to be true. Most people spend more time with their doctors, specialist or therapists than with the Lord in prayer. How can this be?

Don't get me wrong, I am not saying a Christian should not read the newspaper or go to a doctor. Those decisions are up to you. But we have to be so careful not to elevate worldly information and knowledge over the wisdom and truth of God's Word. I personally know people who have memorized the instructions for their medication better than any Scripture. They will recognize all the side effects, but miss the blessings God has promised in His Word. I believe it is time we cry out to God for discernment, for the ability to know whether something comes from Him or not. We must be careful not to believe every voice that speaks to us, but to discern the voice of truth.

If we believe in truth, we should also do as it says. We should be obedient to the teachings of Jesus. In John 8:31-32 Jesus speaks to believers and when we read His words today, they are certainly speaking to us,

So Jesus said to those who believed in him, "If you obey my teaching, you are really my disciples; you will know the truth, and the truth will set you free."

Yes, the truth will set us free. Free from condemnation, free from fear and guilt and shame. Don't we all love this scripture? However, we cannot separate verse 32 from 31. We are really His disciples if we obey His teaching, we will know the truth and the truth will set us free. We cannot expect freedom if we are not willing to obey. Please, let go of the idea that obedience to His commands is an Old Testament idea. The apostle John writes:

If we obey God's commands, then we are sure that we know him. If we say that we know him, but do not obey

his commands, we are liars and there is no truth in us. But if we obey his word, we are the ones whose love for God has really been made perfect. This is how we can be sure that we are in union with God: if we say that we remain in union with God, we should live just as Jesus Christ did (1 John 2:3-6).

He almost spells it out. If we obey, we love God. If we do not obey, we are liars. The truth is not in us. And he furthermore calls for application of that truth: do it, live it! Live as Jesus lived. This is practical Christianity. Don't let anyone tell you that God's commands are outdated or difficult or no longer valid. They show us the heart of God. John pleads with the believers of his time and when we read his words today, they will certainly speak to us,

Everyone who believes that Jesus is the Christ is born of God, and everyone who loves the father loves his child as well. This is how we know that we love the children of God: by loving God and carrying out his commands. In fact, <u>this is love for God: to keep his commands.</u> And his commands are not burdensome (1 John 5:1-4).

Wow, His commands are not burdensome, they should be the delight of our heart. Jesus gave us both the great commandment and the great commission. He told us to love God above all and our neighbors as ourselves and then to go into the world and be the living body of Christ on earth.

I would like to end this book with several scriptures about truth. It will really be helpful and build up your faith when you

- read them aloud,
- meditate on them,
- use them in prayer,
- ask the Holy Spirit to make the words come alive, and
- if possible, to practice (implement) them!

The Spirit of truth, who has taken up residence in your heart, will help you from day to day, from moment to moment. He will reveal the truth about God and give glory to Jesus.

Teach me to live according to your truth, for you are my God, who saves me. I always trust in you (Psalms 25:5). We have this Teacher living in us, the Spirit of truth. We can ask His help to live a life of truth.

Open my eyes, so that I may see the wonderful truths in your law (Psalms 119:18). Sometimes we have been blinded by our upbringing, certain doctrine or teachings and we need to ask the Spirit of truth for revelation knowledge.

A lie has a short life, but truth lives on forever (Proverbs 12:19). Lies will die, but truth will live forever. We can ask the Spirit of truth to help and inspire us to speak words of eternal life and truth over our families, our churches and our nation.

By speaking the truth in a spirit of love, we must grow up in every way to Christ, who is the head. (Ephesians 4:15). Truth without love can be hurtful. We should ask the Spirit of truth to reveal Christ to us in everything we think, say or do.

No more lying, then! Each of you must tell the truth to the other believer, because we are all members together in the body of Christ (Ephesians 4:25). Oh, what an exhortation for the church today. Let us live in truth with one another and no longer hide behind our masks.

They won the victory over him by the blood of the Lamb and by the truth which they proclaimed; and they were willing to give up their lives and die (Revelation 12:11). We can overcome the enemy by the blood of Jesus *and* by the truth we proclaim. We should ask the Spirit of truth to give us the right words to speak when biblical values are being questioned or attacked.

Meditate on the following:

❖ *What is my definition of truth?*

❖ *Have I tolerated unbiblical teachings to change my perspective on truth?*

❖ *How do I usually respond when asked to give an honest answer?*

Journal your thoughts:

Bibliography

Also available in English:

My Neighbor's House, *Digging Deeper to Find the Treasure That will Satisfy the Longing of Your Heart* (2013)

What do we do with the old pages of Exodus 20 in this current age and time? How do we apply them in our daily life? It is one thing to say, "Oh, I don't envy my neighbor, his house, car, or wife. I don't desire what someone else has." But come to think of it, what do you desire? What are the desires of your heart? Are you passionate for the right things?

What does the Tenth Commandment offer to today's society? How can you benefit from its wisdom? The message of God's last commandment is both bold and obvious: don't be envious of others. But that isn't always the easiest thing to do, especially with an American media that bombards us with images of size zero celebrities, lavish mansions, and Louis Vuitton.

In this fifth book in the Ten Commandments series, you'll learn how to desire meaningful things and apply God's word to everyday life. Join Marja as she discovers the spiritual principles behind the Tenth Commandment. The Bible offers answers that can help us to become more practical in living out our faith.

Grace of Giving, *Turning the Key to Enter & Experience Fullness of Life* (2011)

2011 Reader's Favorite Gold Medal Award Winner
'Best Christian Non-Fiction'

It is one thing to claim we do not steal, but the logical next question would be, "What do we do? How do we go from merely obeying such a command to fulfilling it in our daily lives? Is it truly possible to become a cheerful giver?"

In her award-winning book Grace of Giving, the fourth one in this series, Marja answers these questions by taking an in-depth look at the commandment "do not steal." The author offers a liberating and fresh insight on the eighth commandment as she shares how we can leave behind the way of the thief, which always cries for more, more, more. We are programmed to spend most of our lives accumulating possessions whether they are the house, the car, the boat, the job, the money, or the mate we desire. We think this will make us happier and give us a more fulfilled life. How can we shift that all-too-human attitude of gathering into an attitude of giving? In her known step-by-step method, she slowly reveals the way of the Master, which is cheerful, abundant, and costly giving that will lead us into a life in all its fullness!

Grace of Giving is also available in Italian, Spanish, German, Polish and Russian language paper back

Breath of Life, *A Journey into Origin and Purpose of Spirit, Soul, and Body* (2008)

As human beings, we are made in the image and likeness of God. We are uniquely designed triune beings: spirit, soul, and body, yet one. The author takes the reader on a journey to our earthly beginnings and beyond. Based on biblical concepts and a surprising array of scriptures, she has painted an artistic picture of a colorful and loving God who is the source of all life. Breath of life is based on the commandment not to commit murder and it deals with the very core of our existence: life before and after conception.

Respectfully Yours, *Revealing God's Truth about Well-being and a Long Life* (2007)

Respectfully Yours is the second book in a series about the Ten Commandments in the twenty-first century. Based on the commandment to honor our parents, it deals with a much broader aspect of family life—the mutual respect between God, parents, and children. The letter of the Old Testament bursts into life as author Marja explains the new way of the Spirit. This book is not just a short and easy-to-understand study; it is a thought-provoking page turner that will transform your view of the parent-child relationship!

Sacred Sabbath, *God's Way to Multiply Our Time and Restore Our Joy* (2006)

Sacred Sabbath is the first book in a series about the Ten Commandments in the twenty-first century. It is a short and easy to understand study that doles out profound nuggets of wisdom to anyone who wants to live the life God had in mind when He created mankind. It explains how we can fulfill the law in a spirit of love just as Jesus did. Sacred Sabbath will lead the reader into an inward change rather than toward an outward experience.

Visit the author at www.marjameijers.com